Collecting Honey Pot.

John Doyle

BBNO
The Weaven
Little Dewchurch
Hereford
HR2 6PP

ISBN 978-0-905652-08-5

Contents

Foreword

Honey is an international food, and as a result, honey pots are an international commodity - they have been made in countries all around the world. As a result of this, and their long history, different honey pots exist by the thousand. Collecting them has been my passion for the past 12 years, and still I find new ones to add to my collection.

Anyone with an interest in honey pots will know only too well that there is a total lack of information on the subject, bar a few magazine articles over the years. This book, the first ever published on honey pots, sets out to redress this imbalance.

I have painstakingly carried out all the research myself, so that I can be sure that the facts are, as far as possible, correct and accurate.

I hope that you will enjoy this book and it will encourage and help you to set up your own collection.

John Doyle
Chislehurst 2009

Introduction

Definition

WHAT EXACTLY DEFINES A HONEY POT?

A honey pot is an item of tableware from which honey can be dispensed, and which is fashioned or decorated in a way to identify it with the honey bee.

In this way it can be differentiated from a preserve pot.

It can be used with a honey drizzler, or a special 'honey spoon'. The drizzler may be provided as an independent article, or as part of the design of the honey pot. Rarely, a matching or an integral moulded saucer may accompany a honey pot, although those made for the American market are more commonly seen with a separate saucer. This was designed to catch any runs of honey, or to provide a surface on which to rest the drizzler or spoon.

This definition is very simplistic, and from the serious collectors viewpoint there is far more to the definition of a honey pot. This is described in more detail below :-

TYPES AND CATEGORIES

- Beehive : Skep or W.B.C. shaped
- Box
- Bear
- Bee
- Jug
- Miscellaneous

BEEHIVE

The most desirable and collectable honey pots are those based on the shape of an old fashioned, traditional straw beehive. This is known as a skep. It can be a modern artistic interpretation of this basic shape. Such honey pots are usually decorated with bees, although they do not have to be. These bees can be painted, embossed, impressed or three dimensional. A large bee is often moulded to form the decorative knop on the top of the lid, to facilitate easy access to the honey! It may have a drizzler or spoon hole on the side of the lid.

Some honey pots are in the shape of the W.B.C. (William Broughton Carr) hive. They are often in a plain white glaze and decorated with painted bees and flowers.

BOX

Boxes or honey boxes are pots moulded in the shape of a shallow box with a lid. They are often very attractive in design and decoration, and therefore very desirable to the serious honey pot collector. I will go into more detail in the chapter on pottery and ceramic pots.

BEAR

With the obvious connection between bears and their love of honey, many honey pots can be found in the shape of a bear! They range from those based on Winnie the Pooh, to those which are anatomically correct, or comic in their interpretation. They are usually moulded with a skep beehive and bees. Some are just bears with a bee on them, and some a bear moulded on a skep shaped pot. The lids on bear pots are commonly made from the shoulders and head, or from a cut out on their back.

BEE

Some honey pots have been moulded in the shape of an entire bee. The abdomen of the bee holds a reservoir of honey, and the wings form the lid. Metal legs support the body of the bee to complete the honey pot. Some of these bee honey pots exist without legs.

Famous bee honey pots have been made by Mellona (The Netherlands) and by Goebel (Germany).

JUG

Jug 'honey pots' can be found in France, but are almost exclusively an American honey pot item where they are more correctly called honey pitchers. They are moulded with skep cane features, but in the shape of a jug. Honey bees are moulded on them, and the lid can be in the shape of another skep, or flat and adorned with a large bee. Some of these pitchers are stamped with JAPAN. They come in a range of bright colours, some embellished with gold outlines.

MISCELLANEOUS

Honey pots can also be found in a myriad of other shapes. However, to qualify as a honey pot they should as a bare minimum be decorated with the word 'Honey'! They sometimes include a bee in their decoration. Those with just 'Honey' written on them are less desirable to the honey pot collector, and may form a detached secondary collection.

Unidentifiable honey pot are those which were sold containing honey, but not in a way to make then identifiable as such. They may come in any shape or decoration. The only clue may be a sticker on the base, or an attached label. This type of pot, although still a honey pot, is the least desirable. This is also an area for confusion, many are nothing more than preserve pots.

Whatever type or category a honey pot falls into, they all have a very familiar theme when it comes to the representation of the honey bee! Very, very few actually resemble an anatomically correct honeybee. Even with artistic license, I have seen moth like bees, stick insect type bees, and some even looking like winged pigs! Few are decorated in the correct colours.

History of the honey pot

The first honey pots, or more precisely, 'pots' to hold honey, probably evolved early in the days of primitive man (albeit in a very basic form) when he discovered the honey of wild bees, and his need to keep or store this food source. We know of the very early existence of honey bees through ancient cave paintings and carvings and depictions in tombs of the ancient Egyptians. Even the Bible makes many references to honey and the honey bee. Honey is a truly ancient food, having survived right through to the present day. Of course these very, very early pots would bear no resemblance to the decorative honey pots of today- their development was to come thousands of years later, in recently modern times by comparison. I have seen myself, at first hand, a Roman honey pot in a local museum in London. Made from fired clay, it was in the shape of a simple, rimmed pot.

So how did the honey pot evolve into the attractive, sometimes highly decorated item which is the subject of this book?

The first decorative honey pots as we know them first appeared and became commercially available during the Georgian period (1714-1837). They were made in both ceramic and silver. Early ceramic honey pots were made by Wedgwood, and by Chamberlain Worcester. Examples from both manufacturers can be viewed in London's Victoria & Albert Museum in South Kensington, London. Several silversmiths during the period are known to have made honey pots, as examples still survive to this day. However, of these, the most famous and highly regarded is Paul Storr. He was based in London and he made several different designs of silver honey pots. They were all based on the shape of a straw skep, some plain, and some adorned with bees. His honey pots were and are, outstanding- beautifully made and with great attention to detail. It is also possible to see one of Paul Storr's silver honey pots in the silver gallery in the Victoria and Albert Museum. Paul Storr honey pots very occasionally come up for auction, selling for tens of thousands of pounds. Many of the silver and silver plated honey pots in existence today have been based on or influenced by these very early designs.

Of course, these early honey pots would have been very expensive, and only within the reach of the very wealthy. Cheaper alternatives would have also appeared. Examples survive in both silver plate, and in Sheffield plate. These 'cheaper' alternatives would again, only have been in the reach of the wealthy. Wedgwood were probably the first pottery to have produced a honey pot with legs and a stand (or bench) in 1802. Although other manufacturers have produced honey pots with legs, Belleek are singly the most famous company to have produced such honey pots over very many years.

It was only as a result of the Industrial Revolution and the development of techniques in mass production that so many household items became more widely available, and lower in price. Many decorative table items, previously only made in silver, started to appear in pottery and ceramic. They were now in the reach of the Victorian middle classes, and the honey pot was included. Honey pots also started to appear made from pressed glass. Many different honey pots survive from this period to the present day. Some fetch high prices, but some are still well with the reach of the amateur collector.

The heyday of the honey pot was in the 1920s-1930s, an era when life was at a slower, more relaxed pace. Breakfast and teatime during this era is depicted in an idyllic scene : family sat around the table, father at the head! In such times bread and jam, or bread and honey was a very common teatime treat. It was also a time for table etiquette. Jam would be decanted into an attractive preserve pot, and honey decanted from a jar into a suitable honey pot. Incidentally, many of the glass jars of honey from this period were decorative in their own right by today's standards: glass moulded in bands in imitation of a skep, moulded in the shape of a honeycomb, and even embossed with bears. Some of the most treasured honey pots were made during this period – brightly coloured, and with flowers. Clarice Cliff is a name which comes to mind. During this period, and in subsequent years, right up to the present day, there have been few, if indeed any, major pottery manufacturers not including a honey pot in their range. During this time span, there have of course been foreign imports. Japanese pots from the 1920's and 1930's were, and still are, particularly popular.

Today, with modern economic pressures of work and lifestyle changes, the traditional teatime image has long since disappeared in many British homes. Long hours may fragment a family from dining together. Advances in technology and changes in food habits and preparation e.g. by quick cook convenience foods have had an impact. We are also more affluent these days, and we no longer need to eat bread and jam, or bread and honey as an after tea dessert or filler. A whole new market in desserts has evolved over the past 20 years - all have indirectly added to the demise of the honey pot, and few are made nowadays purely for their intended function, to hold honey for the table. The only time of the year you can always find honey pots in the shops, is during the pre-Christmas period when some are produced as part of a gift pack included in supermarket and department stores Christmas gift ranges. Having said that, honey has, and is, enjoying a revival as people become more aware of health issues, and the benefits of honey as a natural food.

Honey pots were not only sold individually or as part of a larger teatime or breakfast service. They were also sold as part of the souvenir trade. Seaside resorts all over the country sold honey pots. The West Country in particular, with its large tourist industry has always sold honey pots, and indeed still does in many of its more busier resorts and attractions. Stately Home and National Trust gift shops have all sold souvenir honey pots. Many of the honey pots sold in this way have actually been made by local potteries, and potted with locally sourced honey. Some souvenir honey pots carry the name from where they were purchased e.g. I have pots emblazoned with 'Bala', 'Buckfast Abbey', 'Looe', and even a Czechoslovakian lustre ware honey pot with 'A Present from Brighton'. Some of these will have come with a jar of honey, some filled with honey, and some filled with sweets.

Overseas honey pots are still produced as part of the souvenir industry in popular holiday destinations like Portugal and Spain. Many of these honey pots can be found in the shape of a Grecian amphora or urn, complete with a lid. They are usually a glazed terracotta clay with the word 'Honey' written in any of a number of languages. Some are glazed white with colourful patterns, and some include a painted bee. (I should point out here that many Portuguese honey pots were exported to the U.K. in the 1960's in an array of colours, and moulded in shapes specifically to appeal to the British market. They were not souvenirs).

Beekeeping is an international industry and so honey is an international food, eaten all over the world. As such, the honey pot is also an international item. The British are not the only people who have given this highly prized food a special place on the table in the form of a honey pot! I have honey pots from Russia, Japan, China, South Africa, Australia, the U.S.A., Canada, Italy, France, The Netherlands, Belgium, Portugal, Spain, Austria, Finland, Israel, India, Norway, Germany, and Bulgaria in my collection. Some honey pots are easily recognisable and attributable to a country by their shape or style, although this should be regarded as a rule of thumb. As already noted, Portuguese and Spanish honey pots tend to be made in the shape of a Grecian amphora or urn; French honey pots tend to have tall, 'stretched' lids, while those made specifically for the French souvenir market tend to be a smaller, basic pot shape, glazed, and sealed with a cork for a lid; German honey pots are painted and decorated with attention to detail; Eastern European (as in the countries that made up the former U.S.S.R.) tend to feature a Bear; American tend to be larger in size and can sometimes feature a bear, or a 'comic' bee; Israeli honey pots can be identified by the word 'Honey' in Hebrew.

When is a honey pot not a honey pot?

I have seen many 'honey pots' appear in antique shops, in online auctions, and indeed in people's collections which are not in fact honey pots! To all intents and purposes they can be identical in appearance and function to a honey pot i.e.

skep shaped, and functional with a removable lid, but were never intended to hold honey.

So when is a honey pot not a honey pot? When it is a sugar bowl, solid perfume or other cosmetic container, money box, sweets container, bath crystal container, jewellery holder, cheese dome, a biscuit or cookie holder, a kitchen storage container, or a preserve pot! I have all such examples of these within my collection! Estée Lauder for example, produced a solid perfume in a gold skep adorned with two bees; Avon produced a 'Honey Bee Moonwind Cologne' in an amber skep bottle with a gold bee on its lid, and Marks & Spencer produced a taller, slimmer ceramic yellow skep covered in bees to contain bath crystals.

Types of Honey Pot

Pottery and ceramic

HONEY POTS

Probably around ninety five percent of any honey pot collection will be made up of ceramic pots made from white or red clay (terracotta) formulated and fired at different kiln temperatures to produce earthenware, stoneware, bone china, earthenware, Parian ware, Jasperware, porcelain etc. The skills of the designer and of the mould maker, the potter who hand throws a pot, precise knowledge of how clay behaves in the kiln, kiln temperatures, formulation of glazes, and the skill of the decorating artist all combine to make the many thousands of different honey pots available.

Some of these honey pots will have been made by leading pottery manufacturers, some by local independent potters. Major British potteries to have produced honey pots include Wedgwood (who have made honey pots in both earthenware and Jasperware), Royal Doulton (and earlier as Doulton), Royal Worcester (and earlier as Chamberlain Worcester), Royal Crown Derby, Spode, Minton, Beswick, Price, Poole, Sylvac, Wemyss, Royal Winton, Shorter, Carlton Ware, Wilkinson and Belleek. Examples of ceramic honey pots made by internationally well known companies include Goebel (Germany), Royal Copenhagen (Denmark), and Nortitake (Japan). Lesser well known companies to have produced honey pots include Frankoma (U.S.A.), Mellona (The Netherlands), Marutomo (Marutomoware) and Maruhon (Maruhonware) both Japanese, Gzhel (Russia), and Lennox (U.S.A.). Some of these companies still manufacture honey pots from time to time. Many new honey pots around the world are currently manufactured in China.

Of all the ceramic honey pots the Japanese ones are probably the most popular and cherished additions to any collection. Name stamps to look for underneath are Marutomoware or Maruhonware. They were manufactured in the 1920's and 1930's and they come in the form of skeps (both cane and honeycomb moulded), as tree trunks, and as round, square or domed cottages. Although not made to a high quality (they were probably cheaply produced and sold) their skep shaped honey pots are attractively decorated in bright, vivid colours, with bees about their body, and a large attractive bee as a finial or knop on their lid. Fairylight, Cottageware and Klimax also produced similar wares to these two companies. Noritake is a Japanese pottery producing very high quality porcelain products. Included have been some very desirable honey pots, finished in a high gloss, or lustre glaze.

The most famous honey pots are probably those of the art deco period made by Clarice Cliff. Again moulded in the shape of a detailed skep, they are brightly coloured in various patterns, with a distinctive Clarice Cliff design bee positioned on the side of the lid.

BOXES

Honey boxes have been been sold and described in a number of different ways: section dish, honey dish, section box, honey box, cut comb box. A section dish or box is designed more specifically to take a section of honey comb directly from the hive. A honey box or cut comb box takes a piece of honeycomb cut to size. Boxes can also include round boxes. Honey boxes or section dishes have, like honey pots, been made by most British pottery manufacturers. They include Poole, Carlton Ware, Bretby, Royal Doulton, Minton, W.H. Goss, Wemyss, Crown Devon and Shorter to note just a few. Shorter produced a section dish in the same design, but in a number of different colourways. The same design was also made by H.J. Wood, and yet other versions carry the stamp of E. H. Taylor, an old beekeeping supplies company. Most comprise of a straightforward shallow box with lid. The lid usually has a large bee as a knop. These bees, like so many on honey pots, rarely, if ever, correctly represent a honey bee. Having said that, Royal Doulton section boxes display a very attractive and detailed bee. Although stylised, the bee knop on Poole Pottery honey boxes is also very attractive. Bees and other decorations e.g. hollyhocks, honeysuckle, clover and other painted flowers and bees can decorate bases, although they can also be plain with no decoration. The main decoration is usually focussed on the lid. These plain bases however, can be found embossed or impressed with honeycomb, bands and wicker designs. Some boxes are moulded with short legs, some with an integral, moulded dish, and some with a separate plate.

Glass

Pressed glass honey pots can date as far back as Victorian times when mass production afforded them at a lower price. Blown or cut glass honey pots possibly existed earlier.

HONEY POTS

Like their ceramic counterparts, glass honey pots have been made in many countries. The majority have been made in clear glass, clear coloured glass, and in coloured opaque glass. Some are opaque with coloured streaks and are known as slag glass. There are some, and these tend to be American, made from milk glass, and from Vaseline glass. Crystal glass honey pots are usually engraved with bees, and modern examples have been manufactured in the U.K., and in the Czech Republic.

The glass honey pots in my collection are all skep influenced in shape. Some of the plainer, clear glass pots pot are moulded as honey cells, and have an integral moulded saucer with a scalloped edge. The skep shaped honey pots are very

A Sylvac (English) honey pot.

A Noritake (Japanese) pot in a lustre glaze.

A Carlton Ware (English) section dish.

A three legged Belleek (Northern Irish) honey pot

Two Japanese copies of Belleek honey pots.

Three hollyhock decorated Marutomoware (Japanese) honey pots.

Four Marutomoware (Japanese) honeycomb impressed pots

Left hand, Marutomoware, right hand Maruhonware. Both Japanese.

14

An assortment of seven section dishes, all British.

Two Belgian pots.

Portuguese 'beaker' honey pots.

Two sets of double pots.
Left hand, stamped 'Occupied Japan', right hand, stamped Marutomoware.

A Lefton (U.S.A.) pot, made in Japan.

Two bear pots, one stamped Japan.

Two Tiara (American) glass boxes.

Two clear glass pots with integral saucer, unmarked.

detailed (as indeed the pressed glass process lends itself to), individual strands of straw can be seen, along with the weave of the skep and bees. Some pots have detailing, or accents, painted on the bees and stand in gold, or other colours. Almost all of these pots have a stand and legs moulded as part of the main body. Those that are stamped include Boyd, L.E. Smith and Imperial Glass, all American companies. I have a number of British made glass honey pots, but like so many made in this medium, they are unstamped. As such, it is impossible to attribute them at the time of writing to a manufacturer.

BOXES

Glass honey boxes are very uncommon in the U.K and Europe, America seeming to be their main home. Some of the older ones manufactured in America are not decorated with bees and would be unidentifiable as honey boxes without prior knowledge. However many are decorated with bees, and nearly all have an integral stand, or feet. The most popular to collect, and therefore most famous, are those sold under the name of 'Tiara' as a 'Tiara Exclusive'. They were made by the Indiana Glass Company in the U.S.A. I believe they were not actually manufactured to hold honey, but they very quickly proved irresistible to honey pot collectors, they are to all intents and purposes a honey box or dish! They are outstanding in their decoration. Tiara boxes are moulded with skeps and many, many bees on the base, sides and lid. The glass came in very many colours, including both clear and opaque colours. Earlier versions were manufactured with differently moulded legs.

Glass honey pots are still being manufactured today, and include an Italian Alessi honey pot designed in 1995 by Theo Williams (glass base with a stainless steel honey drizzler and lid), and a small clear glass skep marketed by M.S.C. International in Montreal, Canada.

HONEY DISPENSERS

Glass honey dispensers also exist. They are made in two parts, the top being the container for the honey. This is usually moulded with a honey cell pattern, and with a stainless steel handle and button. The depressing of the button allows the honey to flow out of the bottom, and the releasing of the button stops the flow. The top then rests into the bottom part.

Silver and metal

Silver honey pots have been in production since the eighteenth century. You will have read in more detail about these at the beginning of this book.

I have only ever seen silver honey pots in the shape of a skep. 'Silver' honey pots include those made of solid silver, silver plate, Sheffield plate, and base metals finished in silver colour. An inner glass liner would have held the honey. They have been made in a number of countries including the United Kingdom of course, America, some European countries (often described by dealers as 'European silver') and Japan, many still influenced by Paul Storr's early pot design. Most come with an integral saucer, and many were also made with a matching silver honey drizzler or spoon. These spoons and drizzlers can be very attractive, and collectable in their own right. However, you should not be put off the purchase of a silver honey pot if it has either of these missing.

More recent examples have been made by contemporary silversmiths and sold at premium prices. This does not mean you cannot include any silver honey pots in your collection. Silver plated pots will be within most collectors' budget, especially in online auctions.

Other metal honey pots exist in chrome, and in pewter.

Wood

HONEY POTS

The majority of wooden honey pots have been made from turned wood in the shape of a skep. Although not as attractive or decorative as their ceramic counterparts, they can have a unique beauty in their own right, in the grain and type of the wood used. Most of these honey pots were made to hold a glass or plastic inner liner. Some were designed and made to hold a jar of honey. The skep is not an exclusive design for the wooden honey pot – they can be cylindrical as well, usually with an accompanying carved wooden bear, both mounted together on a wooden plinth. Sometimes a wooden honey serving spoon may complete the set. These cylinders may be lightly etched or carved with a bee upon them, and sometimes the word 'Honey'. I have an example from Russia, and another that I attribute to being American, possibly made by the indigenous people of North America.

BOXES

Wooden honey boxes exist, but I have only ever seen plain boxes with a shaped knob on the lid. They usually contain a plastic liner in which the honeycomb would have sat.

Plastics

HONEY POTS

Although acrylic plastic has been around for a number of decades, I am unfamiliar with any 'old' honey pots in this or other plastic materials . Some acrylic honey pots may have been made as early as in the 1960's or 1970's. These were clear with a dead bee on a daisy in the lid. They were later reproduced and appeared in abundance in the late 1990's. In this latter issue, their design shape varied considerably: I have examples which are cylindrical, diamond, hexagonal, square, domed and oval. One has an integral saucer, and they all come with a honey spoon. Others have been manufactured very recently where there are several small bees in the lid, made of coloured plastic, and hovering over a flower head. Most of these were made in China and were available for around the five pounds mark.

Other acrylic honey pots exist. Some can have a lid with a hole in the middle, where the honey drizzler handle rests. Others are banded like a skep, but in the shape of a carafe. Boots the Chemist included what to all intents and purposes resembles a banded skep honey pot. It was actually sold as part of their Christmas gift range, filled with Royal Jelly pearls! This important detail has been lost in just a matter of years, and features in many a honey pot collection!

BOXES

I am unaware of any plastic honey boxes.

Collecting Honey Pots

How to start

Most new honey pots collectors start off by purchasing honey brown glazed skep shaped honey pots. Although many of these are decorative and quite attractive in their own right, they are in most collectors taste, the least desirable. Honey pots in any colour other than brown may seem at first to be elusive, but there are in fact far more coloured honey pots in existence, than in brown!

A good way to start your collection is to tell all your family, friends and colleagues that you are starting to collect honey pots. Take an example, if you have one, to show them. This will have the benefit of many, many dozens of eyes looking out for you, and it will eventually pay dividends – I have gained many beautiful honey pots this way! Don't forget to tell them that you will pay them for the pot, and that you don't expect it as a gift. It is important to make this clear, as you don't want your extra pairs of eyes overlooking honey pots because of money issues getting in the way.

There are many different sources from which you can start a collection of honey pots. Charity shops and jumble sales are probably the most local sources. Patience may be needed, as it may take many visits over a period of time before a honey pot turns up. Car Boot Sales and Garage Sales are also a local source. I have spent thousands of hours trawling the stalls at such sales. It can be very hit and miss at times. Sometimes you may find several, sometimes none. Keep in good faith and don't give up. If you see a honey pot, don't rush over to it instantly, and don't appear over keen – such behaviour can be picked-up and you could end up paying more! That's why I prefer a stall with the prices labelled. Don't be afraid to haggle the price down, but don't be unreasonable as sellers have been known – in my case – to withdraw the item from sale! Prices can vary considerably, due to any number of variables, but you could spend anything from fifty pence to several pounds. If it looks like a particularly desirable piece, the cost may be tens of pounds. Unfortunately there will always be the stall holder who thinks they have a really valuable piece, and will try to convince you, even when you know it is quite a common honey pot. In such cases it is virtually impossible to haggle the price down, so it is best left – the seller will learn the hard way.

Auctions, and certainly online auctions are also excellent places to find honey pots. When buying online, make sure that you check a seller's feedback and be sure to read any neutral or negative feedback. Whatever type of auction you bid at or on, have a maximum figure in your mind and try to stick to it as there are extras payable beyond the final, or hammer price. At an auction this may include a buyer's premium and VAT, online it will include postage and packaging. The advantage of auctions where you attend in person is that you can inspect the pot yourself before bidding. The advantages of an online auction is that you are obviously in the comfort of your own home, and you have a range of honey pots from which to choose to bid on. There are disadvantages specific to online auctions: you are totally reliant on the accuracy of the sellers description, and visually, by photographs. Most sites however provide the facility to email the seller if you have more specific questions, and this should be taken advantage of if you are in doubt about any aspect of the pot. I must say that I have been buying from online auctions for nearly ten years and have had few problems. They have been a source of great enrichment for my collection. Problems that I have experienced include pots arriving smashed, items incorrectly described, and in the case of one item, it not turning up. Where items have arrived smashed, it has always been through bad packaging on the part of the seller. Either no packaging had been inserted between the lid and the base, or too small a box was used which resulted in insufficient filler packaging to absorb any impact during transit. I received one ceramic honey pot recently wrapped in a piece of bubble wrap, and then inserted in two Jiffy bags. Amazingly, and against all odds, it arrived in perfect condition! Where honey pots have arrived broken, I have found all sellers to be very helpful, offering a compromise, or giving a full refund. If the pot is particularly expensive then it is wise to ask the seller to quote you for the Special Delivery postal rate. In this way it will be insured against breakage. Where a honey pot was incorrectly described, a refund was offered to me. I wanted the pot for my collection – it was very rare - and I managed to negotiate by email a discount, and the seller sent me a cheque. The item which failed to turn up was from an overseas seller. The seller ignored my emails. I complained to the auction site, and shortly after the seller was banned from the site. I did lose my money however. Having said that, I have made many other purchases from overseas with no problems. Whilst talking of purchasing from overseas, it should be borne in mind that when bidding for honey pots on sites outside of the E.U., the purchase may be subject to import tax.

If you are prepared to look further afield then Antique shops, centres, and fairs are all good hunting grounds. If a dealer asks what you are looking for it is good to tell them, if they have a honey pot which is not on obvious display, you'll be glad they asked you. If you become a regular, dealers in my experience are always very happy to keep a look out for you when they are out sourcing stock, another way of boosting your collection.

The final source is that for brand new honey pots – from normal high street shops! China shops, department stores, gift shops, kitchenware shops and delicatessens are all good places to look. In London's Piccadilly there is a very famous shop, famous for being the Queen's grocer. It is called Fortnum & Mason. This store alone has given the honey pot collector many fabulous pieces over many decades, and from leading, collectable potteries. All the major, national supermarket chains have, and still do, produce honey pots as part of their Christmas gift ranges as do stores like Marks & Spencer, and Boots the Chemist. Department stores like Harrods, Harvey Nichols and Selfridges have also produced honey pots in the past. It Is well worth visiting some of these stores to see if they are currently including honey pots in their food departments.

Brand new honey pots can also be found in pottery studios or shops. My car will stop automatically and do a u-turn if I pass a pottery! When you are visiting an independent pottery and you cannot see any honey pots, ask if they would be prepared to paint any pots in their existing stock to your own individual specifications. Make sure that you give them very precise details, as they will only paint what you want. At the other extreme you could ask them to produce a honey pot for you using their own artistic licence. Some potters may be prepared to make a mould from an old honey pot if you provide this. But be warned, your original honey pot may be broken in the mould making process, and in any case, it will be a very expensive exercise.

Honey pots can vary in price considerably, from pence for an ordinary brown honey pot, to tens of thousands of pounds if it is a rare silver honey pot.

As you gain experience in your collecting, and your collection increases in size, you will notice that some honey pots are very similar, if not identical to one another. You may also notice that their decoration or glaze is very different, and that there is a different stamp on the base. Many honey pots have been copied over the years as their design registration has expired. Some have even been manufactured from an old original pot. Such examples will be identical in so far as their size-they will be slightly smaller versions. Care when purchasing such pots must be exercised. I have an example of a white honey pot, correctly stamped on the base. An identical version exists in brown without a base stamp. The brown pot is often labelled and sold as being manufactured by the same pottery as the white pot, when in fact it is not. As a result a premium price is being asked for a pot which is not actually what it appears to be! This is probably not intentional, but knowledge is to your advantage in such cases. Even sought after Clarice Cliff honey pots fetching hundreds of pounds at auction are being copied.

When purchasing expensive honey pots from any source, remember the adage 'Caveat emptor', or 'Let the buyer beware' and make sure you have made a mental note of my check list!

CHECK LIST

1. Always scrutinize the wings of the bee. These are the most vulnerable part of the pot. Check for chips, restoration and in particular, re-glued wings.

2. 'Ping' the side with your finger. You should hear a ringing sound. A thud, or muffled sound should immediately arouse suspicion, there may be cracks, not readily visible to the eye.

3. Only be tempted to buy a damaged honey pot if it is cheap, or in your view only, exceptional.

4. Expect to pay more for pots which overlap with other collecting categories e.g. a Poole collector may be after a honey pot purely because it is from that pottery.

5. Check that the pot has the correct lid. Lids are sometimes paired up with the wrong base, whether on purpose or not. If you are unsure, go by your instinct. Some slight variation in glaze colour is common.

6. Always ask for a best price. It is normal for dealers to give at least a 10% discount on pots over £10. Do your best!

7. As with all antiques and collectables, paying by cash can often result in higher discounts.

8. Make sure you get a receipt. If you are buying a particularly collectable or expensive pot, ensure these details are on it. If your Clarice Cliff turns out to be a cheap imitation, you could have redress with a detailed receipt.

9. If your pot contains honey, empty it as soon as possible. Honey can sometimes stain a pot, and sometimes leak from under the lid.

Displaying

The most obvious way to display your honey pot collection is in a glass cabinet, behind closed doors. Shelves are fine, but your bee's wings will quickly acquire fur coats, no matter how clean you are! I do not favour older china cabinets. They are often stacked with widely spaced shelves, wasting a lot of space in between (after all most honey pots are only several inches or centimetres high). Having plate glass shelves cut to size to fix in between the existing shelves is a solution, although it is not cheap. You would be better investing the money in more suitable cabinets. I have found the best glass cabinets to be those designed for the storage and display of C.D.'s. Most honey pots fall just short of the height of a C.D. and this maximises the use of space. Stores such as Ikea and Argos regularly include such cabinets in their ranges. If your pots are to be on open display out of the relative safety of a cabinet, then it is important to place your pots so that they cannot be easily knocked. It is also a good idea to secure the lid to their base, a very vulnerable part of your honey pot, especially with the delicate bee wings. Clear sticky tape is a quick and easy solution, although it is not the best method. It can be seen, and will discolour with time leaving a sticky residue. Sticky tape should only be used on a plain glazed pot, or pot where the decoration is under glazed, otherwise removal of the tape could remove part of the decoration. A far better solution is Blutak. Small balls stuck on the inside rim of the pot base will securely hold the lid in place, and without being visible.

Having decided in what to display your honey pots, you will then have to decide how to actually display them. You may choose to display them by country e.g. all Japanese pots on one shelf, or one cabinet, German on or in another, and so on. Honey pots can also be displayed by design, by manufacturer, by material, or by colour. Groups of yellow honey pots, blue honey pots etc. look particularly attractive.

Care and repair

It is my personal opinion that honey pots are best handled as little as possible to avoid any accidental chips or breakages. Having said that, even those honey pots displayed behind glass in a cabinet, will eventually need cleaning. I find the best way to do this is with a soft damp cloth. It should have been soaked in a diluted washing up liquid solution, and well rung out. If your honey pot is made of any sort of porous material, or the surface is porous, take great care or you may find you cause irreparable damage. In such case a light dusting with a dry, soft paint brush may be more appropriate. Under no circumstances would I ever recommend immersing any of your pots in water, apparent 'glazes' can bubble and peel off. A damp cloth in my experience is ideal and there is no need to dry with a towel. It is equally effective on glass, wood and plastic. Tarnished silver pots will require a polish, and I would recommend a proprietary silver cleaner in the form of a wadding.

What should you do if the unthinkable happens and you damage one of your pots? If the break is clean, then gluing is the first obvious solution. Glues specifically designed for ceramics can be used, but ordinary super glue works equally well. In order to make it work, you will need to lightly dampen with a wet cotton bud the porous unglazed edges you want to stick together, before applying the super glue. It should then adhere with no problems. If the damage is greater, or where a piece cannot be found, you may need to remodel a part. An excellent product called Milliput exists. It is an epoxy putty which can be used as a filler, or moulded to make a new bee wing, for example. Professional restorers are known to use this product. It comes in several colours and is available from craft shops. Obviously repairs will need to be painted or touched up with a matching colour. Acrylic paints are good. For a final glossy glaze, clear nail varnish may provide a satisfactory result.

Record Keeping

It is a good idea to keep a record of your honey pots whether in a book, a folder, or on a computer. Entries can include the date purchased, the manufacturer, a brief description, and the price paid. You may also want to include from where you purchased it, and a column to add a valuation. Digital cameras, and photographic records are another way in which you can keep a record. You may want to 'record keep' by attaching a small sticker on the base of each pot with similar details on, or by putting a small note inside each individual pot. Receipts should always be obtained with your purchase, and these in themselves can become a simple form of record keeping. If you purchase from an internet auction, a print out of the sellers page is yet another form of record.

The European Honeypot Collectors' Society

Having started collecting honey pots with great fervour, I quickly became frustrated at the lack of information on the subject. There were no books – this is the first – and the internet was in its infancy, so there was nothing to be found online either. In 1998 I decided to start a collectors club from scratch : The European Honeypot Collectors' Society, which I still run today. Incidentally the misspelling of 'Honeypot' was deliberate. I managed to arrange publicity through several antique, collecting and beekeeping magazines, and membership took off. Later a Channel 4 programme, Collectors Lot approached me, and the Society's annual swap meet was featured along with a collection belonging to a member. As a result of this broadcast membership rose sharply!

The aims of the Society are simple :

- To promote and encourage interest in honey pots.

- To be the leading authority on the subject.

- To bring together those with an interest in honey pots by meeting socially, and to share information in order to learn from one another.

- To be a non-profit making organisation.

In addition, the Society is open to anyone who has a genuine interest and enthusiasm for honey pots, regardless of their geographical position.

Later I built a website for the Society, and posted it on the internet at

www.geocities.com/tehcsuk

I publish a monthly four page newsletter 'The Honeypot', with one page in full colour featuring the collection of a member. An annual swap meets is held, where hundreds of colourful honey pots are to be seen, swapped and purchased. An exclusive annual honey pot is produced, as are exclusive limited editions.

Full details can be found on the website or by writing to me at The European Honeypot Collectors' Society, The Honeypot, 18 Victoria Road, Chislehurst, Kent BR7 6DF. United Kingdom.

Front cover: *A Wedgwood Jasperware honey pot*

Back cover: Top: *An assortment of honey pots including British, Japanese, Portuguese and Italian.*

     Bottom: Two Fielding's Crown Devon pots in a lustre glaze.

Index